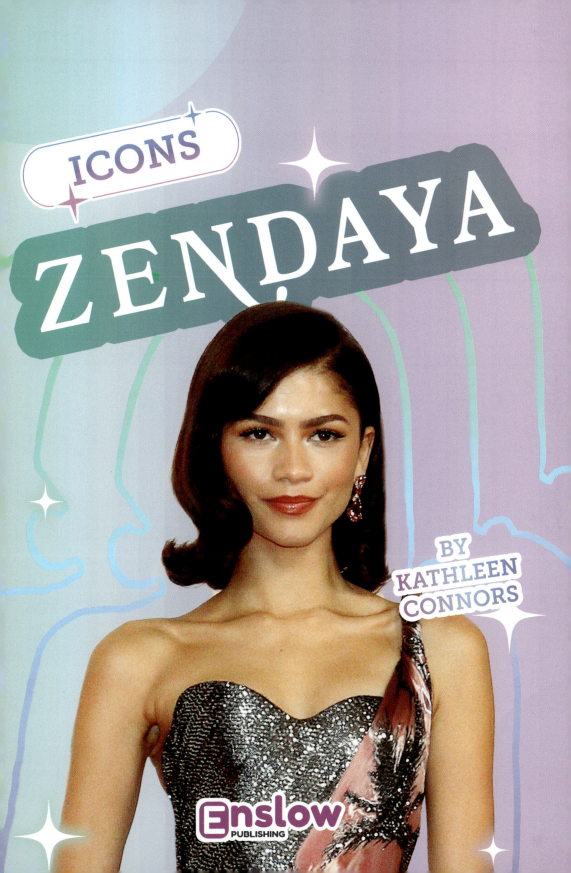

ICONS
ZENDAYA

BY KATHLEEN CONNORS

Enslow PUBLISHING

Please visit our website, www.enslow.com.
For a free color catalog of all our high-quality books, call toll free 1-800-398-2504 or fax 1-877-980-4454.

Cataloging-in-Publication Data
Names: Connors, Katheleen.
Title: Zendaya / Katheleen Connors.
Description: Buffalo, NY : Enslow Publishing, 2026. | Series: Icons | Includes glossary and index.
Identifiers: ISBN 9781978544635 (pbk.) | ISBN 9781978544642 (library bound) | ISBN 9781978544659 (ebook)
Subjects: LCSH: Zendaya, 1996---Juvenile literature. | Actresses--United States--Biography--Juvenile literature. | Singers--United States--Biography--Juvenile literature. | Models (Persons)--United States--Biography--Juvenile literature.
Classification: LCC PN2287.Z47 C66 2026 | DDC 791.4302'8092--dc23

Published in 2026 by
Enslow Publishing
2544 Clinton Street
Buffalo, NY 14224

Copyright © 2026 Enslow Publishing

Designer: Tanya Dellaccio Keeney
Editor: Kristen Rajczak Nelson

Photo credits: Cover Geisler-Fotopress GmbH/Alamy Images; p. 5 Paul Smith/Alamy Images; pp. 7, 13 WENN Rights Ltd/Alamy Images; pp. 9, 21 PictureLux/The Hollywood Archive/Alamy Images; p. 10 Kathy Hutchins/Shutterstock.com; pp. 11, 23 Album/Alamy Images; p. 15 WENN US/Alamy Images; p. 17 Entertainment Pictures/Alamy Images; p. 18 Pictorial Press Ltd/Alamy Images; p. 19 Hyperstar/Alamy Images; p. 24 BFA/Alamy Images; p. 25 Doug Peters/Alamy Images; p. 27 Sipa/USA/Alamy Images; p. 29 Tinseltown/Shutterstock.com.

All rights reserved. No part of this book may be reproduced in any form without permission in writing from the publisher, except by a reviewer.

Printed in the United States of America

CPSIA compliance information: Batch #CSENS26: For further information contact Enslow Publishing, at 1-800-398-2504.

Contents

WOMAN AT THE TOP 4
GROWING UP 6
DISNEY DIVA 10
ON THE BIG SCREEN 16
HARDWORKING ACTRESS 20
FASHION ICON 26
STANDING UP 28
TIMELINE 30
FOR MORE INFORMATION 31
GLOSSARY 32
INDEX 32

Words in the glossary appear in **bold** the first time they are used in the text.

Woman at the Top

Zendaya is one of Hollywood's top **icons** today! She's known for her stylish red-carpet appearances and many TV and movie **roles**, from the Disney Channel to *Dune*. Her work has earned her millions of fans!

ICONIC!

Zendaya told *Allure* in 2020: "I think my fans pretty much understand me. They know I don't leave my house, they know that I'm lazy, they know that I'm pretty open but also pretty **private**."

Growing Up

Zendaya was born on September 1, 1996. She grew up in Oakland, California. Her mom, Claire Stoermer, and her dad, Kazembe Ajamu Coleman, worked as a teachers. She has three older sisters and two older brothers.

ICONIC!
Zendaya has often said her mom is the person she looks up to most.

Kazembe Claire

7

Zendaya has been **performing** since she was very young. She studied acting and was part of a hip-hop dance group. Her mom worked at a theater that put on plays by William Shakespeare. Zendaya learned a lot from watching them! She acted in plays too.

ICONIC!

Zendaya worked as a model when she was a child.

Disney Diva

In 2010, Zendaya began to put her dance moves to work on the Disney Channel show *Shake It Up*. She starred in the show with Bella Thorne. Zendaya played Rocky Blue. *Shake It Up* put Zendaya in the spotlight! The show ended in 2013.

Bella Thorne

Zendaya in Shake It Up

ICONIC!

Zendaya was only 14 when she started starring in Shake It Up.

Zendaya wanted to make music too. She put out "Replay" in 2013. It was the first single, or song, from her album *Zendaya*. It made the *Billboard* Hot 100! *Zendaya* came out in September 2013.

ICONIC!

Zendaya danced her way to the finals of Dancing with the Stars in 2013. She came in second!

Zendaya began to star in another Disney Channel show in 2015. *K.C. Undercover* aired for three seasons. When the show ended in 2018, Zendaya was 21—and starting to break out of being a child star.

ICONIC!

Zendaya felt a lot of pressure as a teen actor. She told Vogue she felt she had to be "this perfect being, and be everything that everyone needs me to be."

On the Big Screen

In 2017, Zendaya starred as a **trapeze** artist in *The Greatest Showman*. She not only learned trapeze, but also sang in the role. "Rewrite the Stars," the song she sang with co-star Zac Efron, was a hit!

ICONIC!

Zendaya has appeared in many music videos, including Taylor Swift's video for "Bad Blood" that came out in 2015.

Zendaya in The Greatest Showman

Zendaya reached even more fans as MJ in *Spider-Man: Homecoming,* which came out in 2017. She played the role again in 2019 in *Spider-Man: Far from Home.* She won a People's Choice **Award** and a Kid's Choice Award after those movies!

ICONIC!

In 2016, Zendaya was named to the Forbes *30 Under 30* list, a list of young people from around the world who are talented in their area of work.

Hardworking Actress

The show *Euphoria* pushed Zendaya more than anything she'd done before. She played Rue Bennett, a teenager with a drug problem, among other issues. The show came out in 2019. Fans and **critics** alike thought Zendaya was great in it!

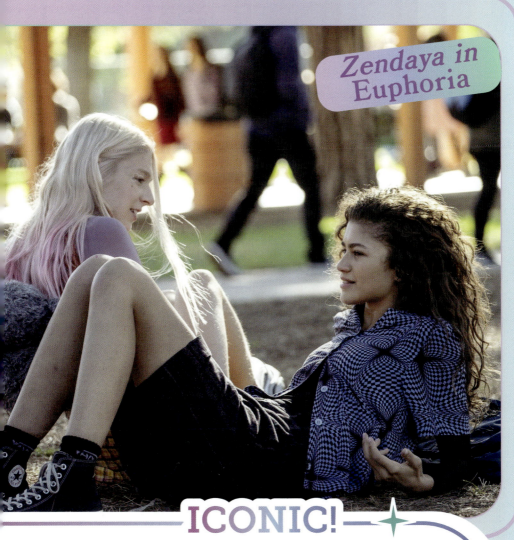

Zendaya in Euphoria

ICONIC!

Zendaya won an Emmy Award for outstanding lead actress in a **drama** after both season one and season two of Euphoria. She is the first Black woman to win this Emmy twice!

Zendaya continued playing MJ in *Spider-Man: No Way Home,* which came out in 2021. She hit the big screen again that year in *Dune: Part One.* Zendaya played Chani. She said of making *Dune*: "It felt cool and so exciting to be part of the magic."

ICONIC!

Zendaya did the voice for Lola Bunny in Space Jam: A New Legacy, which came out in 2021. She has voiced characters in other movies too, including Smallfoot.

Zendaya in Dune

Dune: Part Two came out in 2024. Zendaya gave her all to her role, wearing a heavy costume and filming in the heat. She had also spent a long time preparing for her other movie of 2024: *Challengers*. She played a tennis star!

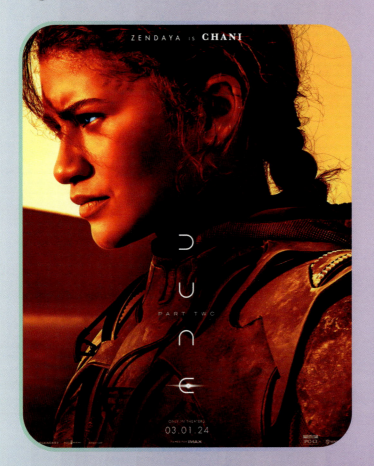

ICONIC!

Zendaya had never played tennis before. She got ready to play Tashi in Challengers by learning the game as well as copying the footwork of real tennis players.

Fashion Icon

Zendaya has fun with fashion! She's known for bright colors, clothes having to do with her movie roles, and trying out different hairstyles. She also has become the face of high-end brands, including Lancôme and Valentino.

ICONIC!

In 2019, Zendaya worked with Tommy Hilfiger to create Tommy x Zendaya. She made sure the clothes could be worn by people of all shapes and sizes.

27

Standing Up

Zendaya wants better **representation** for people of color in Hollywood, especially Black women. Her dream is to direct someday and be part of hiring all kinds of artists to work with. With all this icon has done so far, her dream is sure to come true!

ICONIC!

In 2020, Zendaya said: "The only way that doors are going to continue to be open [is] if we keep [asking] people that look like us, and other people who don't look like us, to come through the door."

Timeline

1996	Zendaya is born in California.
2010-2013	She stars in Shake It Up.
2013	The album Zendaya comes out.
2015-2018	Zendaya stars in K.C. Undercover.
2017	She appears in The Greatest Showman and Spider-Man: Homecoming.
2019	Spider-Man: Far from Home comes out. Zendaya begins starring in Euphoria.
2021	Dune: Part One and Spider-Man: No Way Home come out.
2024	Zendaya stars in Dune: Part Two and Challengers.

For More Information

BOOKS

Bleckwehl, Mary E. *Zendaya*. Mankato, MN: Amicus Learning, 2025.

Katie, Kawa. *Zendaya: Making a Difference as a Movie and TV Star.* Buffalo, NY: KidHaven Publishing, 2025.

WEBSITE

Zendaya
https://www.zendaya.com/
Keep up with everything Zendaya is doing on her website.

Zendaya - IMDb
https://www.imdb.com/name/nm3918035/
Find out what Zendaya is up to next on her IMDb page.

Publisher's note to educators and parents: Our editors have carefully reviewed these websites to ensure that they are suitable for students. Many websites change frequently, however, and we cannot guarantee that a site's future contents will continue to meet our high standards of quality and educational value. Be advised that students should be closely supervised whenever they access the internet.

Glossary

award: Prize.

critic: Someone who makes judgements about something, such as a piece of art or writing.

drama: A movie or show not meant to be funny.

icon: A person who is very successful and admired.

perform: To act, play music, or sing.

private: Staying out of the public eye.

representation: The way a TV show, movie, book, or other media deals with and presents age, gender, or ethnicity.

role: The part a person plays.

trapeze: A bar that hangs from two ropes. It is used to do gymnastic tricks in midair.

Index

awards, 18, 21
California, 6, 30
Challengers, 24, 25, 30
dance, 8, 10, 12
Disney Channel, 4, 10, 14
Dune movies, 4, 22, 24, 30
Euphoria, 20, 21, 30
family, 6
Greatest Showman, The, 16, 30
K.C. Undercover, 14, 30
Shake It Up, 10, 11, 30
Spider-Man movies, 18, 22, 30
Zendaya (album), 12, 30